SK

CITIES OF THE
WORLD

BERLIN

BY R. CONRAD STEIN

CP CHILDREN'S PRESS®
A Division of Grolier Publishing
New York London Hong Kong Sydney
Danbury, Connecticut

CONSULTANTS

Peter Hayes, Ph.D.
Alfred W. Chase Professor
Department of History
Northwestern University

Linda Cornwell
Learning Resource Consultant
Indiana Department of Education

The heraldic bear used as an icon throughout this book is the symbol of Berlin.

Project Editor: Downing Publishing Services
Design Director: Karen Kohn & Associates, Ltd.
Photo Researcher: Jan Izzo
Pronunciations: Courtesy of Tony Breed, M.A., Linguistics, University of Chicago

---

NOTES ON German PRONUNCIATION

The words in this book are pronounced basically the way the pronunciation guides look. There are a few notes, however: *ah* is like *a* in father; *a* is as in can; *ar* is as in far; *ai* and *ay* are like *ai* in rain; *aw* is as in draw; *ow* and *aow* are always as in cow, never as in tow; *u* and *uh* are very short and quick, like *a* in about; *igh* is as in light. The sound *h̲* does not occur in English. It is like the *h* in hat but stronger and harsher. If you try to say *k* as in kite but relax and slur the sound, it will sound like *h̲*. *Pf* sounds exactly as it is spelled, like *pf* in cupfull.

Library of Congress Cataloging-in-Publication Data
Stein, R. Conrad.
      Berlin by R. Conrad Stein.
            p.   cm. — (Cities of the world)
      Includes index.
      Summary: Describes the history, culture, people, daily life, and points of interest of Germany's major city.
      ISBN 0-516-20582-X
      1. Berlin (Germany) — Juvenile literature.   [l. Berlin (Germany)]
I. Title. II. Series: Cities of the world (New York, N.Y.)
DD860.S829   1997   96-50147
943'. 155—dc21   CIP
                                                AC

TABLE OF CONTENTS

The Brandenburg Gate stands as a proud symbol of Berlin. The graceful archway was built in 1791. At the time, Berlin was a walled city. The Brandenburg Gate was its grand entrance. In modern times, another wall was built just a few feet from the Brandenburg Gate. It was a wall of shame that split this German city in half. In the fall of 1989, that wall came tumbling down to the thunderous cheers of Berlin's people.

The Brandenburg Gate, shown above in a nineteenth-century colored drawing, is crowned by the Quadriga *(below), a sculpture of the Greek goddess of Victory riding her chariot.*

Berliners have endured war, starvation, and isolation. How did they survive one crisis after another? Ask them. First, Berliners will tell you they have learned to laugh at trouble. Germans often describe the famous Berlin humor with the word *Schnauze,* meaning "sharp wit." Second, Berliners say the air above their city has a certain chemistry that energizes them. It is called *Berliner Luft* ("Berlin air"). Whatever the reasons, Berliners enjoy a special spirit. Visitors, too, are entranced by this wonderful city and its people. All guests are welcome. Just pass under the Brandenburg Gate.

This colorful section of the Berlin Wall near the Brandenburg Gate stands as a memorial to the once-divided city and to the people who lost their lives trying to leave East Berlin. The entertainer in the foreground has become a favorite subject for picture-taking tourists.

Schnauze (SHNAOWT-SUH)
Berliner Luft (BAIR-LEE-NAIR LOOFT)

*I*t is difficult to find a genuine Berliner. The town is largely full of foreigners, who make it a lively place.

— A VISITOR TO BERLIN,
WRITING IN THE YEAR 1820.

THE MANY FACES OF BERLIN

Some 700 years ago, Berlin was made up of two tiny villages on opposite sides of the River Spree. Craftspeople and traders carried on lively businesses in the two towns. Foreigners flooded in hoping to share in the prosperity. First came the French Huguenots, who sought religious freedom. Jews, Poles, Swiss, and Austrians followed the French. Berlin developed a separate character from neighboring towns. The blond-haired "German" look was less evident on the streets. Berliners spoke with a distinct accent. Fellow Germans came to regard Berlin residents as a breed apart. Writing more than 200 years ago, the great German poet Johann Wolfgang von Goethe called Berliners "that saucy race."

Today, too, immigration has changed the face of the German capital. It is estimated that only half its residents are natives of the city. The others come either from different parts of Germany or from foreign lands. People of about 150 different nationalities live and work in modern Berlin. Immigrants include Greeks, Italians, Yugoslavs, Afghans, and Turks. The foreign-born people tend to have more children than do the Germans. One in four of the city's children under six years old have parents born in foreign lands.

Spree (SHPRAY)

An eighteenth-century picture of Berlin and the River Spree

On this page: The
many faces of Berlin

Turks are the largest foreign group. Berlin has the biggest Turkish community found anywhere outside Turkey. Turks began arriving in the early 1960s. At the time, Germany desperately needed workers. The Turks did the dirty jobs. They scrubbed dishes in restaurants. They toiled over machines in factories. Many set up tiny businesses. Turkish-owned shoe-repair shops popped up everywhere. Berliners developed a taste for shish kebab, which Turkish cooks sold from pushcarts.

Then, the once-rosy employment picture changed. By the 1980s, Germans had to compete with Turks for jobs. Parents complained that Turkish children were overcrowding the schools. Some Turks also soured on German life. Most Turks are Muslims. They objected to their daughters wearing skimpy swimsuits at high-school pools. Fights broke out between young Turks and German teenagers who called themselves "skinheads." The skinheads wore close-cropped haircuts. They claimed to revere the German World War II leader, Adolf Hitler. Many older Berliners had little love for the Turks, but shook their heads in disgust at the skinheads. The older residents remembered the misery Adolf Hitler had brought to their city.

Turkish girls in Berlin's Kreuzberg neighborhood

Adolf Hitler (AH-DAWLF HIT-LER)
Kreuzberg (KROYTS-BERK)

Little Istanbul

An old working-class neighborhood called Kreuzberg holds the city's largest concentration of Turkish immigrants. Here, women stroll the sidewalks wearing the traditional head scarf called a *higab*. Men wear a Muslim hat called a *takke*. Five times a day, prayers can be heard drifting from the neighborhood mosques. Berlin has more than twenty-five mosques (Muslim houses of worship).

Muslim women wear head scarves in public, but not in the privacy of their homes.

WALL OF THE MIND

World War II left Berlin divided into two cities: East Berlin and West Berlin. For years, the ugly Berlin Wall stood, splitting east from west. The wall is now gone. Berlin is one city again. But a wall of the mind remains.

Berliners use the term *Ossis* to describe one-time East Berliners and *Wessis* for West Berliners. When said in anger, the terms are insulting. For example, former West Berliners say Ossis are lazy and lacking in ambition. East Berliners, on the other hand, claim the Wessis are pushy and arrogant. In the old days, West Berlin had a capitalistic economy. East Berlin had a Communist system. Without question, the people of West Berlin enjoyed a higher standard of living. West Berliners owned powerful automobiles. Many East Berliners drove a puttering two-cylinder car called a Trabant. At full speed, the Trabant sounded like a lawn mower.

Before the reunification of Berlin, many East Berliners drove two-cylinder Trabants that looked like this.

A West Berlin school playground near the Berlin Wall

Ossis (AW-SIZ)
Wessis (VEH-SIZ)
Trabant (TRAH-BAHNT)

Wessis (former West Berliners) enjoy gathering at sidewalk cafes on the Ku'damm (left).

Most Ossis (former East Berliners) prefer to meet at the squares and parks in what used to be East Berlin (below).

Even today, Wessis and Ossis tend to live in separate societies. Ossis still gather at Alexanderplatz, which was once East Berlin's major public square. There, the Ossis complain that reunification has brought crime and unemployment to their district. It is true that many state-owned factories in the east have closed. However, Wessis say those Communist-era factories were inefficient. The favorite hangouts for Wessis are the restaurants in the Kurfürstendamm District (commonly called the Ku'damm). There, Wessis gripe about increased taxes. The new taxes are caused by unemployment payments to residents of the east. Tax money is also used to repair broken-down highways and railroads in the eastern section.

Despite the east-west split, most Berliners agree that reunification was a blessing. But in the mid-1990s, a strange T-shirt made an appearance in the city. The message on the front of the T-shirt was dismissed as an example of the Berliner Schnauze (humor). It said, "I want my wall back."

THE GREEN CITY

Berliners say they keep their good humor by frequently escaping to the country. In their case, the country lies only a subway ride away. Berlin is a huge city, sprawling over 341 square miles. In area, it is six times larger than Paris. Within its boundaries are 50 square miles of lakes, parks, and forests. On the outskirts are working farms. Remarkably, nearly 7 per cent of Berlin's land area is used for agriculture. On the outlying farms, one sees cows munching on grass in the very shadows of high-rise apartment buildings.

This fountain in one of Berlin's many parks is a popular place to rest, chat with friends, or play.

Weekend picnics are a long-standing Berlin tradition. Families fill baskets with homemade potato salad, bread, and sausages. The family dog usually comes along. Estimates say Berliners own 100,000 dogs. This is one of the largest canine populations in Europe. On picnic grounds, children kick soccer balls. In the spring, they fly kites. A family with a little money will take their sailboat out to one of the city's major lakes. Working-class people fish from the shores.

Family picnics are a long-standing Berlin tradition.

An excursion boat on the Spree River

The German capital is built on water. Two wide rivers, the Havel and the Spree, wind through its heart. The river system creates fifty large lakes and more than 100 ponds. In years past, sadly, the water was polluted with factory and sewer discharges. Recently, a government crackdown on polluters has opened many waterways to sports and pleasure. Berliners can now choose to swim from 31 bathing beaches. The Strandbad Beach on Lake Wannsee is said to be the largest inland bathing beach in all of Europe. Space is carefully allotted at Grunewald Lake. One beach there is assigned to families. A nearby beach is reserved for people who like to swim with their dogs. A faraway beach is used for nude bathing.

Havel (HAH-FULL)
Strandbad (SHTRAHND-BAHT)
Wannsee (VAHN-ZAY)
Grunewald (GROO-NU-VAHLT)
Pfaueninsel (PFAOW-UH-NIN-SUL)

Berliners and visitors alike enjoy rides on tour boats, which cruise along the rivers. Passengers sit on the decks, relax, and watch the scenery glide by. Food and beer are served on-board. Riverboats frequently pass under bridges. Water-laced Berlin has more than 1,600 bridges. The boats often stop at one of the city's 35 islands. Many of the islands are uninhabited and serve as conservation areas. At Pfaueninsel (Peacock Island), visitors are greeted by a flock of peacocks.

On picnics and cruises, Berliners leave the tension of the big city behind. Since Berlin has a wealth of parks and woodlands, a family outing in the country can take place nearly every weekend. The frequent outings keep smiles on the faces of Berliners.

Markisches Viertel
(MAIR-KISH-ESS FIHR -TULL)

This peacock feather may have come from one of the birds on Pfaueninsel.

A Desperate Need for Housing

Although Berlin has ample parks, it suffers a dismal housing shortage. Many people have migrated from the country to the German capital in recent years. As a result, the city is at least 100,000 apartments short of the demand. Huge high-rise developments such as the Markisches Viertel, built in the late 1960s, house up to 60,000 people. Architectural critics denounce the faceless concrete projects as "vertical slums."

For two centuries, the Brandenburg Gate has been a silent witness to historical events. Soldiers—from Napoleon's guards to goose-stepping Nazis—have marched under the archway. The hated Berlin Wall once stood nearby. The Brandenburg Gate has survived the city's many crises. The spirit of the Berlin people is very much like the great gate. Despite the upheavals of history, Berliners will endure.

Nazi (NAHT-SEE)

THE TROUBLESOME POLITICIAN

In the late 1920s, Germany was an impoverished nation. The people still felt the sting of Germany's defeat in World War I (1914–1918). In the early 1930s, the worldwide economic depression hit the country very hard. From out of this despair, Adolf Hitler and his Nazi Party gained popularity. Hitler blamed government officials and Jewish bankers for the nation's problems. The Nazi leader was a spellbinding orator. Huge crowds came to hear his speeches. Yet Berlin, the capital of Germany, was cold to Hitler and his followers. Berlin was Germany's intellectual center. Most educated Berliners saw Hitler as a troublesome politician who hoped to capitalize on the gloomy times. A 1932 election enabled Hitler to take power in Germany—but three out of four Berliners voted against him in the election.

mark (MAHRK)

Because money was worth so little during the 1920s, this news vendor kept her bills in a laundry basket.

The Price of Despair

A crippling currency inflation struck Germany in the 1920s. The cost of a loaf of bread zoomed to 1 million marks. Paper money became next to worthless. The government printed additional zeros on existing 10- or 100-mark notes. Berliners went to stores carrying baskets of marks and returned with only enough food to prepare lunch for the family.

Throughout the 1930s, Hitler consolidated his power by jailing his enemies. Hitler's special targets were the Jews. At the encouragement of the Nazi Party, signs appeared on many Berlin restaurants: "No entry for Jews." On the evening of November 9, 1938, gangs of brown-shirted Nazis stormed through Berlin's streets. The Nazis beat up Jewish people and broke the windows of Jewish-owned stores. Forever after, that night was called *Kristallnacht* (Crystal Night), so named for the shards of broken glass covering the streets.

In later years, the Nazis launched a terrible program of Jewish extermination. We now call the program and its disastrous results the Holocaust. During the Holocaust, some 6 million European Jews, as well as other "enemies of the state," were killed. Berlin Jews tried to survive by masquerading as gentiles or hiding in basements. Still, thousands of Berlin Jews were taken to concentration camps where they were worked to death or executed.

Left and below: Stunned Berliners gaze at the broken glass that covered the streets after Kristallnacht.

Kristallnacht (KRISS-TAHLL-NACHHT)

Nazi leader Adolf Hitler was rising to power in 1929.

Hitler had a strange relationship with Berlin. On the one hand, he had a grandiose plan for the city. The Nazi chief dreamed of building a domed stadium in Berlin large enough to seat 150,000 people. Rising above the stadium would be a triumphal arch. He would even change the name of the capital city from Berlin to Germania. His glistening new city would stand as the headquarters for a great German empire. On the other hand, Hitler disliked and distrusted Berliners. In Berlin, people still talked politics in the cafes. Ideas flowed freely. Fresh ideas frightened the Nazis. A Nazi newspaper denounced

Berlin as a "melting pot of everything that is evil—drinking houses, cinemas, Communism, Jews . . ."

On September 1, 1939, Hitler's armies invaded neighboring Poland. World War II in Europe began.

Above: Hitler's troops celebrating their takeover of the government in 1933 with a torchlight parade through Berlin's Brandenburg Gate
Right: Hitler's motorcycle units driving through a destroyed Polish village in 1939

Germania (GAIR-MAH-NEE-UH)

BERLIN UNDER SIEGE

Most Berliners shunned the Nazi Party. However, they did have faith in the German Air Force, the *Luftwaffe*. The Luftwaffe was the world's most powerful air force. Surely, it would protect the German capital. Then, on the night of August 25, 1940, a small group of British bombers made its way to Berlin. Berliners heard the frightening wail of air-raid sirens. They saw long fingers of searchlight beams probing the skies. People on the streets ran for shelters. That first raid did very little physical damage. But it shattered the city's morale. American reporter William Shirer was stationed in Berlin at the time. He wrote, "Berliners are stunned. They did not think it could ever happen."

Hitler declared war on the United States in December 1941. At the same time, he began losing to his eastern enemy, Russia. By the winter of 1944, Berliners had lost count of how many major air raids they had suffered. The people dreamed up names for sections of their city that had been flattened by bombs: "Craterfield," "Rag Village," "Nothing Left." Before the war, Luftwaffe commander Hermann Goering made a boast. He said if bombs ever fell on the German capital, his name would not be Goering. Instead he would be called Meyer, a common Jewish name. As the raids increased, Goering refused to be seen in public because Berliners taunted him with shouts of "Herr Meyer! Herr Meyer!"

During bombing attacks, Berliners crowded into tiny underground shelters. Some prayed, some wept, others tried to sing. Above them, a deadly rain of bombs pounded their city. All knew a direct hit

These Berliners took refuge in an air-raid shelter during a World War II bombing attack.

Above: Russian tanks rumbling through the streets of Berlin in April 1945 signaled the end of World War II in Germany.
Right: By the end of the war, very few buildings in Berlin had survived. These people were happy to find a place to live, even though it was in a bombed-out building.

Luftwaffe (LOOFT-vah-fuh)
Hermann Goering (HAIR-mahn GOOH-ring)
Herr (HAIR)

would cause their shelter to cave in, burying them alive. A raging fire in the buildings above meant the shelter dwellers would die of asphyxiation. Through the war years, bombs destroyed half the buildings in Berlin and caused 100,000 casualties.

In April 1945, Berliners heard the thunder of artillery rumbling out of the east. Then, tanks followed by Russian infantrymen rolled through the streets. For four years, Russia and Germany had been locked in furious combat. During the war-

torn years, German soldiers had committed many outrages on the Russian people. Now, Russians took their revenge on the civilians of the German capital. The troops shot people in their homes and looted goods. During this terrible battle, Adolf Hitler hid

inside a thick-walled bunker in central Berlin. He waited until enemy soldiers were less than 200 yards away. He then put a pistol to his head and shot himself. On May 2, 1945, the Russian army occupied Berlin. World War II in Europe ended.

AN ISLAND CITY

Grimly, Berliners worked to rebuild. The war had cut the city's population almost in half. More than 70 percent of Berlin's people were now female. Clearing the debris fell to the *Trümmerfrauen* (the rubble women). Those hardy women carried buckets of bricks and ashes from the streets. The women dumped the refuse in such a way as to create mountains of rubble. Later, grass and trees were planted on these mountains. The mounds became a part of the Berlin landscape.

At the end of the war, the victorious nations divided Germany. The Western allies—the United States, Britain, and France—occupied the western half. Russian armies occupied the east. Berlin, too, was split in half. Thus, two separate countries—East Germany and West Germany—emerged. The one-time capital of Germany became two cities: East Berlin and West Berlin.

The Trümmerfrauen worked hard to clear the rubble from the streets of Berlin so the city could be rebuilt.

Trümmerfrauen (TREH-MER-FRAOW-UHN)

West Berlin was an island city. It was situated 100 miles inside the borders of Communist East Germany. In June 1948, Communist soldiers blocked all railroads and highways leading to West Berlin. The United States defied the blockade by flying in supplies. Food, medicine, and even the coal needed to heat apartments was delivered by planes. The supply planes landed and took off at the rate of one a minute. Pilots battled foul weather and operated out of dangerously small airfields. The operation, called the Berlin Airlift, saved the city. In May 1949, the Communists lifted the blockade.

By 1960, more than 1,000 East Germans were slipping over to West Berlin each day. Once in West Berlin, the easterners could fly to other parts of West Germany. There, they could begin a new life free from Communism. In August 1961, the Communists ended this escape route by building a

wall separating the two cities. When completed, the concrete wall stood 15 feet high. Like a great scar, the Berlin Wall snaked through the heart of the old city and stretched into the farming regions on the outskirts. Barbed wire topped the wall. On the eastern side was a cleared area called No Man's Land. Standing along No Man's Land were guard posts. Guards were ordered to shoot on sight anyone who tried to scale the wall.

Above: Berlin Airlift supply planes brought food, medicine, coal, and other necessities of life to the city's people between June 1948 and May 1949.

Below: In August 1961, the Soviet Union, which controlled East Berlin, began building the "Wall of Shame," which divided the city for 28 years.

Yet people tried. Some tried to rush over No Man's Land and climb the wall with ladders. Others tried to tunnel under the barrier. Some even attempted to soar over the wall on hang gliders. The wall stood for 28 years. The many who escaped despite the wall became folk heroes in West Germany. But at least 170 people died attempting to cross the wall that all Germans came to despise.

In 1989, East Germans held angry demonstrations to demand greater freedom of travel. Communist leaders were forced to open the wall at the Brandenburg Gate on November 9. The people completed the wall's destruction. With hammers and chisels, they whacked at the barrier that had divided their city for so long. As the wall crumbled, men and women held great chunks of it over their heads in triumph. East and West Berliners stood on the wall's ruins hugging each other. The next day, a Berlin newspaper printed the headline: BERLIN IS BERLIN AGAIN.

Germany became Germany once more. A year after the wall fell, East Germany and West Germany reunited. Berlin again was made Germany's capital.

A souvenir chunk of the Berlin Wall

Shortly after the Berlin Wall was opened in one spot, Berliners began to destroy the rest of the wall. East German border guards looked on as this man hacked away at the wall with a huge hammer.

Fireworks exploded over the Brandenburg Gate when Germans celebrated the reunification of their country on October 3, 1990.

The Berlin Wall as Art

In divided Berlin, graffiti artists used the west side of the wall as a canvas. Much of the graffiti contained slogans demanding that the wall be torn down. The grimmest of the messages had the names and sometimes the pictures of East Germans who had been shot while trying to escape to West Berlin. Many of these pictures were placed at the exact spot where the escapee had been killed.

Fellow Germans claim that Berliners walk faster than other people. It is said that they also work harder on the job and in school. Even in leisure hours, Berliners are on the move. They devote their spare time to pursuing the arts, playing sports, and having fun at festivals.

A PASSION FOR THE ARTS

The Reichstag Building in Berlin is the official meeting place for the German Parliament. In 1995, a Bulgarian-born artist named Christo launched an unusual project. Christo (he never uses his last name) wrapped the Reichstag in silver fabric. Were Berliners shocked to see this somber building wrapped up like a lunchtime sandwich? A reporter asked people on the street. Some thought it was a novel idea to wrap the Reichstag. Others thought it was a stupid idea. But no one was shocked. Berliners love art. They believe all artists have a right to create.

Reichstag (RIGH<u>H</u>-SHTAHK)

In 1995, artist Christo wrapped the Reichstag in silver fabric.

A great artistic explosion captured Berlin in the 1920s. During the Golden Twenties, German expressionist painters created canvases that were ablaze with color. However, many of the expressionists' pictures were painfully harsh. One expressionist was Otto Dix, who lived for years in Berlin. Dix painted scenes of crippled war veterans begging for coins from upper-class operagoers. Berlin's music halls were alive with fresh works in the 1920s.

Concert lovers flocked to see *The Threepenny Opera*, which portrayed the lives of thieves living in the Berlin underworld. Adolf Hitler and the Nazis put an end to this bright artistic period. Hitler, himself a failed artist, thought Berlin's modern art was too negative for the German state he wished to build.

An Otto Dix painting called Big City

The Reichstag

Built in 1894, the Reichstag has had a troubled history. In 1933, it mysteriously caught fire. Hitler blamed the fire on the Communists and used it as an excuse to arrest Germany's Communist leaders.

Today, creative Berlin flowers once more. Some 300 art galleries display paintings and sculptures. The music scene is one of the most diverse in Europe. Open-air jazz festivals and folk-music concerts are held in the Tiergarten. The Berlin Philharmonic, founded in 1882, is one of the world's finest symphony orchestras. The city has 400 theater groups. About 50 special children's theater companies entertain kids. Also, the capital is bursting with street artists and street entertainers. On Oranienburger Strasse (street), artists paint people's portraits for a small price. In a plaza called Breitscheidplatz, jugglers and acrobats work their magic. Some jugglers keep three or four burning torches in the air. Acrobats toss each other skyward and perform amazing flips. When their acts are over, the street entertainers pass a hat hoping to collect a few coins.

Tiergarten (TEER-GAHR-TUNN)
Oranienburger Strasse
(OH-RAH-NYUNN-BOOR-GAIR SHTRAHSS-UH)
Breitscheidplatz (BRIGHT-SHIGHD-PLAHTS)

When their acts are over, street entertainers like this musician on the Kurfürstendamm (right) usually pass a hat (above) to collect coins.

An educated populace keeps Berlin's art scene vibrant. Three major state universities stand in Berlin. Other academies specialize in the teaching of music, dance, film, art, and architecture. These institutions give Berlin a student population approaching 150,000. Some 10,000 college professors live and work in the city.

Students as well as older Berliners fill the cabarets, taverns that feature entertainment. The cabaret tradition dates back to the 1920s. Anything goes in these special taverns. Musical acts include men dressing as women and women as men. Actors portray political leaders as ignoramuses or incompetents. Given freedom, the artistic expression of a Berliner knows no limits.

Performers in a Berlin cabaret

An organ-grinder at the Brandenburg Gate

cabaret (KAB-UH-RAY)

THE LIVELY WORLD OF SPORTS

In the summertime, Berlin parks are full of skateboarders, inline skaters, and joggers.

Be careful when you walk in a Berlin park. No, you don't have to worry about being attacked by a mugger. Street crime is rare. But inline skaters and children on skateboards dart at you from every direction. Walkways roar with skates. Joggers also pound the pavement in parks. No need to worry about them. Joggers are easy to dodge.

Blame the Berliner Luft, the special snap in the capital's air. It makes Berliners industrious at work. It also energizes them at play. Few other cities boast such wide and varied sports facilities. Each of the capital's 23 boroughs has at least one public swimming pool. Some pools are elaborate and feature sauna baths and wave machines. Boating and fishing are popular in this city, laced by rivers. The coming of winter does not dampen the spirits of sports lovers. Frozen ponds create playgrounds for thousands of ice-skaters. Believe it or not, Berlin has five ski slopes within the city limits.

Tobogganing is a favorite wintertime activity for both children and adults. A slope at Teufelsberg (Devil's Mountain) sends tobogganists on a breathtaking roller-coaster ride. Teufelsberg is a debris mountain. It was created by the rubble women who cleaned up the city after World War II. During the summer months, hang-gliding enthusiasts use Teufelsberg's steep sides as launching pads.

Above: Children use figure skates like this on the frozen ponds in Berlin's parks.

Left: The pool at this ultra-modern sports center is always full of swimmers.

Teufelsberg (TOY-FULLSS-BERK)

The joy of sports helps to unite a once-divided Berlin. Soccer is the city's most passionately followed spectator sport. Soccer matches are held at Berlin's Olympic Stadium, built for the 1936 Olympic Games. In 1990, West Germany (the country was still officially divided then) won the World Cup Soccer Championship. The World Cup is held every four years. It is the Olympics of the soccer world. East Berliners cheered for the West German team as noisily as if it were their own. Gymnastics ranks a close second among

West German teammates celebrate after their first goal during the 1990 World Cup Soccer Championship games.

Berlin's sports fans. East Germany used to produce many great gymnastic performers. All Berliners today crowd into the sports palace once built by the Communists in the eastern section. There, everyone applauds the gymnasts who now represent a united Germany.

Soccer (above and below) is Germany's most popular sport. Gymnastics is a close second.

Left: A summer
festival in Berlin
Below: A typical
Oktoberfest costume

FAIRS AND FUN

Few Berliners have ever milked a cow. Fewer still have dug potatoes
out of the ground on a hot day. Those are the tasks of farmers.
Berliners work in factories or in offices. Still, the people celebrate
Oktoberfest (October Festival). Traditionally, the October Festival
takes place in an open field in the Charlottenburg neighborhood.
There, Berliners sing, dance, and stuff themselves with food. But
wait a minute! Oktoberfest is supposed to be a farmer's holiday.
It gives thanks for the fall harvest. Why should the city dwellers
act so wild over the end of the harvest season? Don't ask. To
Berliners, any excuse to hold a party is accepted. By the way,
the Oktoberfest isn't even held in October. The celebration
begins in mid-September.

The outlying town of Werder holds a Blossom Festival in the spring. The Berlin *Rocksommer* is held in the Treptow neighborhood—to the delight of the city's rock music fans. People attending the festivals drink rivers of the traditional German beverage—beer. Berliners often flavor their beer with a dash of raspberry juice. The concoction, called a *Weisse mit Schuss*, is a Berlin specialty. Small children at the festival drink the raspberry in the form of a soft drink, minus the beer. Berlin's International Green Week Fair features food from all over the world. Guests at the Green Week Fair use the occasion to eat huge quantities of any food they desire.

The International Film Festival

Every February, Berlin hosts the International Film Festival. It is one of the largest such events held anywhere in the world. During the festival, new films are introduced and old ones enjoy revivals. With more than 130 movie houses, Berlin is Germany's film capital. Come early if you want to see a movie here. Theaters are often packed long before the movie starts.

This young Berliner is enjoying one of the city's many festivals.

Oktoberfest (AWK-TOH-BURR-FEST)
Charlottenburg (SHAR-LAWT-UN-BOORK)
Werder (VAIR-DER)
Rocksommer (RAWK-ZOH-MER)
Treptow (TREPP-TAWFF)
Weisse mit Schuss (VIGH-SUH MITT SCHOOSS)

This Berlin waitress is about to serve her customers their order of hearty German food.

Right: A German family enjoying a home-cooked meal

Below: A favorite German dessert is Black Forest cake, a rich chocolate cake with generous fillings of whipped cream, cherries, and chocolate mousse.

Of course, a Berliner needs little excuse to indulge in good-tasting food. Eating habits present a strange contrast in the Berlin character. On the one hand, Berliners are fitness fanatics. Witness their zeal for sports of all kinds. Then observe a Berlin man or woman at one of the city's many wonderful restaurants. A typical meal starts with liver dumpling soup. Next comes roast pork and buttered potatoes, all covered with simmering gravy, and peas with bacon. After finishing the heavy main dish, the Berliner will dig into dessert. How about a generous slice of Black Forest cake—a many-layered chocolate cake with cherry, chocolate mousse, and whipped cream filling? The dangers of fatty foods are generally ignored in this capital city. Few people let worries about diet spoil their fun.

Olof-Palme-Plat

Take a deep breath of the Berliner Luft when visiting the German capital. The air above this city is believed to pep people up. You'll need extra pep to see even a small portion of what this great town has to offer a visitor.

MUSEUMS

No other city in the world can rival Berlin's Museum Island. Lying between two arms of the Spree River, Museum Island is a complex of museum buildings. They include the National Gallery, the Pergamon Museum, and the Bode Museum. Artworks displayed in the complex range from modern paintings to 5,000-year-old Egyptian vases. A Greek altar dating from 160 B.C. is a highlight at the Pergamon Museum. The five buildings on Museum Island are grand examples of nineteenth-century architecture. The structures were damaged during World War II, but underwent painstaking restoration.

Museum Island lies in what was formerly East Berlin. In the old days, travel restrictions made it difficult for a West Berliner to visit the island.

The National Gallery, on Museum Island

The Huguenot Museum

So West Berliners built their own museums. One museum complex rose at Dahlem. A new wing of the Dahlem Museum holds West Berlin's finest art treasures. The rival cities also built two zoos and several sports palaces. Now, east and west are one city again. Yet the old museums and other facilities still stand. For visitors, this duplication is a blessing. It gives people twice as many things to see.

Museums in the capital embrace every imaginable subject. For hundreds of years, Berlin has been a city of immigrants. The Huguenot Museum displays the history of French Huguenots who came here long ago. Many recent immigrants follow the Islamic religion. They visit Berlin's Museum of Islamic Art. The Museum of German History is housed in a monumental building constructed in 1695. Berlin's Natural History Museum features a brachiosaurus. It is the largest dinosaur skeleton on display anywhere in the world. The Dahlem Junior Museum offers exhibits that invite children to touch, feel, and climb upon them.

Dahlem (DAH-lemm)

Checkpoint Charlie

The Museum of Checkpoint Charlie tells the sordid history of the Berlin Wall. Checkpoint Charlie was once a military outpost manned by Allied soldiers. The outpost stood near the Brandenburg Gate. It is now a small museum that displays photos of the wall, photos of escape tunnels, and a car with a secret compartment that was used to hide escapees fleeing from the east.

THE PARKS

No park is more beloved than the Tiergarten. Covering 630 acres, the Tiergarten was once a private hunting ground for German kings. Today, it is a playground dotted with lakes, flower gardens, and groves of trees. Some 19 miles of paths invite long walks. On Sundays, the park is crowded with frisbee throwers, bike riders, and Turkish families gathered around barbecue stands. Berlin's most popular zoo stands in an arm of the Tiergarten. The zoo is close to a business district. Office workers eat lunches in front of cages of lions and frolicking monkeys.

Treptow Park lies in the eastern sector of the city. An annual fireworks display called "Treptow in Flames" has been

Women on a Berlin park bench

Rehberge (RAY-BAIR-GUH)
Wedding (VEDD-ING)

held there every year since 1825. A lovely bridge leads to an island in the Spree. The island serves as an amusement park. It has a Ferris wheel and an open-air children's theater. Treptow was once East Berlin's main park. A massive statue in the park shows a Russian soldier smashing a Nazi swastika beneath his sword.

Rehberge Park offers such activities such as lawn bowling, golf, and winter tobogganing. It even has a fitness trail. Rehberge lies in an interesting neighborhood called Wedding.

Years ago, Wedding was an industrial slum. Its residential buildings were filthy and crowded. Its factories belched smoke. Today, Wedding's factories produce high-tech computers instead of heavy machinery. Young and educated people have moved into what were once slum tenements. Still, new and old neighborhood residents crowd into the park. Everyone enjoys picnics under shade trees at Rehberge. Neighborhoods change in character, but in Berlin, parks are eternal.

"Is this still Berlin?" That question is often asked by visitors entering the Grunewald Forest. The answer is yes, and the question is valid. The Grunewald Forest is a huge expanse of country that lies within the city limits.

Nowhere in all the world is there a city park quite like Grunewald. It covers more than 15 square miles. The forest is thick with birch and pine trees. Hiking trails allow people to walk for hours through woodlands and never see a car. Bordering Grunewald is a large lake formed by the River Havel. The Grunewald Forest is an amazing blend of the country and the city.

LANDMARKS

In 1945, war-torn Berlin was a shambles. Many stately old structures were beyond repair and had to be bulldozed. New buildings went up on their grounds. When possible, older buildings were repaired. In this way, time-honored architecture was preserved. The Kaiser Wilhelm Church (built in 1895) was severely damaged during the war. Berlin authorities decided to leave the shell of the building as it was. In 1961, a new church was built alongside the ruined structure. Thus, the old Kaiser Wilhelm Church stands as a reminder of war's horrors. The new church represents Berlin's rebirth from the rubble.

The Schauspielhaus Theater is a remarkable building that stands in a dramatic architectural setting. The theater, built in 1821, features a peaked roof and a broad staircase. On

This Berlin cityscape shows the ruined Kaiser Wilhelm Church in the background, right.

either side are two magnificent churches. Rising in front is a white marble statue honoring the beloved German playwright Friedrich Schiller. The churches, the statue, and the theater combine to make up Gendarmenmarkt Square. This square was once hailed as Europe's most beautiful plaza. In 1945, the plaza was a battleground. Its buildings were nearly leveled when Russian artillery blasted at German riflemen who were firing from windows. Only in recent years have workers completed rebuilding Gendarmenmarkt Square. Now, the plaza can again take its place as one of Europe's finest.

Patrons at this outdoor cafe have an excellent view of the Kaiser Wilhelm Church.

The Schauspielhaus Theater, in the Gendarmenmarkt

Kaiser Wilhelm (KIGH-ZER VILL-HELM)
Schauspielhaus (SHAOW-SHPEEL-HOWSS)
Friedrich Schiller (FREE-DRIHH SHILL-ER)
Gendarmenmarkt (GEHN-DAHR-MEHN-MAHR<u>HT</u>)

A towering landmark is the Victory Column that rises over the Tiergarten. Completed in 1873, the column celebrated Prussian victories over Denmark and Austria. Some sections of the column contain enemy gun barrels that were captured in battle. Nearby is Bellevue Palace, another architectural treasure. Beyond the Tiergarten spreads a tree-lined boulevard called Unter den Linden. The name means Under the Linden Trees. Before World War II, Unter

The Victory Column rises over the Tiergarten.

Unter den Linden
(OON-ter dain
LINN-dunn)

den Linden was the city's grandest boulevard. After the war, it became the heart of East Berlin. Now, Unter den Linden is the pride of a new and united Berlin.

Rising above Unter den Linden is the Brandenburg Gate. Many tours of Berlin end at this lofty structure. The Brandenburg Gate has witnessed Berlin's destruction, its rebuilding, its division, and its reunification. It now faces Berlin's future. Once more, Berlin is the capital of Germany. And it is again one of the world's great cities.

A view of Unter den Linden with the Berlin Cathedral in the background

Getting Around

When touring the city, visitors are advised to take the subway, the *U-Bahn*, or the elevated train, the *S-Bahn*. Both transit systems are fast, clean, and safe to ride. The trains serve nearly every part of the city. In some neighborhoods, the elevated *S-Bahn* has rows of small shops built under its tracks.

U-Bahn
(OO-BAHN)
S-Bahn
(ESS-BAHN)

FAMOUS LANDMARKS

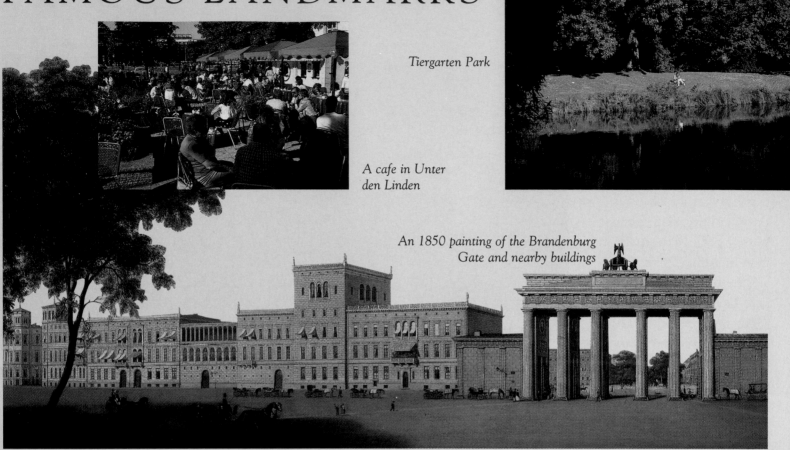

Tiergarten Park

A cafe in Unter
den Linden

An 1850 painting of the Brandenburg
Gate and nearby buildings

Unter den Linden

This historic boulevard is 200 yards wide and runs about three-quarters of a mile. In the 1500s, it was a bridle path leading from the king's palace to the king's private hunting grounds (present-day Tiergarten Park). In 1647, rows of linden trees were planted along both sides of the avenue. It has since been called Unter den Linden— "Under the Lindens."

Brandenburg Gate

Built between 1788 and 1791, the Brandenburg Gate was one of 18 gates in the old city wall. It is the only one that still stands. In 1793, the gate was crowned with a statue titled *Quadriga*, a scene of the Greek goddess of victory riding her chariot. The Brandenburg Gate, severely damaged during World War II, was repaired in 1957.

Tiergarten

One of the pleasures of strolling in this huge park is to gaze at its collection of statues and other monuments. *The Goethe Monument* honors German poet Johann Wolfgang von Goethe (1749–1832). *The Composer Monument* was built in 1904 to celebrate the great German musicians Haydn, Mozart, and Beethoven. During World War II, the trees in the park were chopped down to provide fuel for freezing Berliners. After the war, more than a million trees and saplings were donated from other parts of Germany and Tiergarten was reforested.

Humboldt University

Lying in what was once East Berlin, Humboldt University is an architectural gem built between 1748 and 1753. Over the years, famous scholars, including Georg Hegel and Albert Einstein, have taught or studied at this university. Also here as students were the brothers Grimm, authors of "Hansel and Gretel" and the other *Grimm Fairy Tales*.

Bode Museum,
on Museum
Island

Humboldt University

A modern church
tower stands next to
the shell of the Kaiser
Wilhelm Memorial
Church on the
Kurfürstendam.

Museum Island
Unique in all the world, Museum Island is a complex of museum buildings all concentrated on an island in the River Spree. Sculpture, paintings, and ancient pottery are on display in this most unusual setting.

Alexanderplatz
Today, Alexanderplatz is a pedestrian plaza surrounded by shops. In the 1800s, it was a marketplace, in the early 1900s a shameful slum, and in recent years it was the heart of East Berlin. "Alex," as the people call it, remains a popular gathering place for former East Berlin residents. In the center of the plaza is a 30-foot-tall global clock that displays the time everywhere in the world.

Kaiser Wilhelm Memorial Church
In the western section of Berlin, two churches stand side by side. One is the 100-year-old Kaiser Wilhelm Memorial Church, which was damaged beyond repair during World War II. The old church is a shell that stands 207 feet high. Originally, its tower was 370 feet tall. Alongside it is a new church tower built in 1961. The towers stand together as a symbol of Berlin's recent past—war and rebirth, old and new architecture.

Kurfürstendamm
This 2 1/2-mile boulevard is Berlin's classiest shopping street. Department stores, shops, pricey restaurants, and posh hotels line the street. The "Ku'damm" is a "mustn't miss" for visitors.

Olympic Stadium
Adolf Hitler looked upon the 1936 Olympic Games as a way to showcase the athletes of his German state. To further impress the world, he built the grand Olympic Stadium in Berlin. But the star of the games was African-American runner Jesse Owens, who won four gold medals in track. The Olympic Stadium—which seats almost 100,000 spectators—remains a splendid place to watch soccer games and other sporting events.

FAST FACTS

POPULATION

Metropolitan Area: 3,433,695
Berlin is Germany's largest city as well as its capital.

AREA   341 square miles

CLIMATE Berlin enjoys a generally mild climate, although the city may experience bitter cold spells during the winter months. The average January temperature is 35 degrees Fahrenheit; the average July temperature is 74 degrees Fahrenheit. The summer months are the rainiest time of the year.

INDUSTRIES About half of Berlin's workers hold jobs in factories. The city's factories produce electrical machinery, chemicals, clothing, and processed food products. Berlin is Germany's largest source of jobs for construction workers. Half the city's workforce is devoted to service jobs—advertising, banking, teaching, and managing small shops. With 145 banks, Berlin is one of Europe's most important financial centers.

CHRONOLOGY

1307
The town of Kölln and the town of Berlin merge; previously, the two had been separate towns on opposite sides of the River Spree. The resulting single town is called Berlin.

1710
Berlin numbers 61,000 inhabitants, including many French Huguenots.

1791
The Brandenburg Gate is completed as part of a wall surrounding the city.

1806-1808
French soldiers under Napoleon Bonaparte occupy Berlin.

1819
Berlin's population is 200,000.

1838
The city's first railroad links Berlin with nearby Potsdam.

1871
Berlin becomes the capital of the newly proclaimed German empire.

1918
World War I ends with Germany's defeat.

1934
Adolf Hitler declares himself *führer* (leader) of Germany.

1936
The Olympic Games are held in Berlin.

1939
World War II begins with Germany invading Poland.

Young and old enjoying the fresh air in a park on Tauentzien Strasse.

1940
The British Air Force launches its first air raid on Berlin.

1945
A huge land battle rages on the streets of Berlin between the German army and Russian forces; Hitler commits suicide in his bunker in central Berlin; World War II in Europe ends; Allied forces divide Germany and Berlin.

1948
The Communists blockade West Berlin, forcing the Western Allies to supply the city from the air; the blockade lasts 11 months.

1953
East Berliners riot in protest of Communist rule.

1961
The Communists build the Berlin Wall through the heart of the city.

1989
After massive demonstrations, the Communists open a portion of the Berlin Wall; demonstrators tear down the remaining sections.

1990
East and West Germany reunite.

1991
Berlin again becomes the capital of Germany.

BERLIN

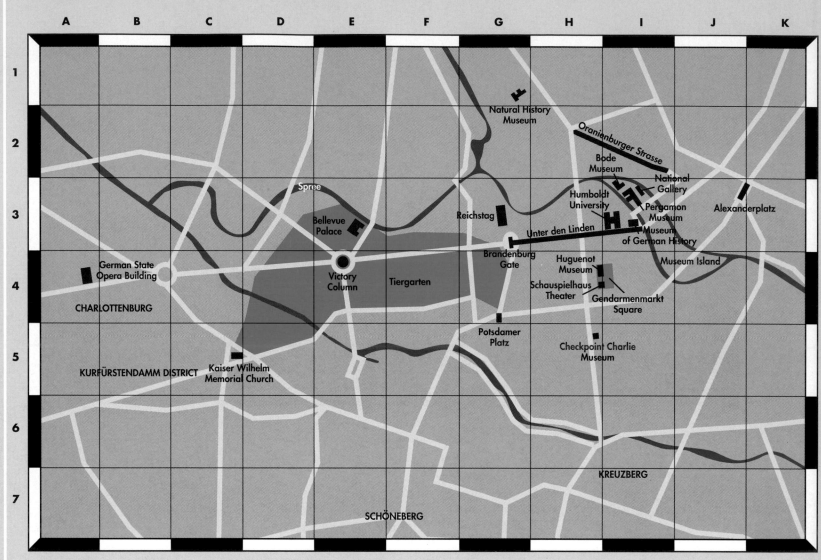

L   M   N   O

1

Markisches
Viertel

WEDDING

Rehberge Park

2

Olympic
Stadium   Europa
Center   BERLIN   Strandbad
Beach

Teufelsberg

Havel

Grunewald
Forest   Grunewald
Lake   Treptow
Park

3

■ Dahlem Museum
Complex
and
Museum of Islamic Art   TREPTOW

Lake
Wannsee

Peacock
Island

4

BERLIN AND SURROUNDINGS

GLOSSARY

bunker: A small fort or fortress

canine: Having to do with dogs

graffiti: Names, messages, or advertisements drawn or spray painted on walls without permission

grandiose: Overly ambitious

gripe: Complain

Huguenot: A French Protestant group of the sixteenth and seventeenth centuries

ignoramus: An ignorant person

monumental: Grand and glorious

orator: A speaker

Prussian: A person from Prussia, a former German state

residential: Living quarters

sauna: A steam bath

shish kebab: Cubes of marinated meat and vegetables cooked and served on long rods called skewers

siege: The act of surrounding a town or fort in order to capture it

sordid: Dirty, evil

symbol: An object that represents something else, such as a feeling or an idea

taunt: To mock or jeer at

vibrant: Throbbing with energy or life

zeal: Great enthusiasm

Picture Identifications

Cover: Brandenburg Gate, girl in local costume, toy Trabant car
Page 1: Berlin schoolchildren
Pages 4-5: Brandenburg Gate illuminated at dusk
Pages 8-9: A Berlin flower market
Page 9: Turkish children in Berlin
Pages 20-21: French Emperor Napoleon I marching into Berlin on October 27, 1806
Pages 32-33: Children at Berlin's Neptune Fountain
Pages 46-47: Entrance to the Zoological Gardens

INDEX

Page numbers in boldface type indicate illustrations

TO FIND OUT MORE

BOOKS

Ayer, Eleanor H. *Berlin*. Cities at War series. New York: New Discovery Books, 1992.

Burke, Patrick. *Germany: Modern Industrial World*. New York: Thomas Learning, 1995.

Dudman, John. *The Division of Berlin*. Vero Beach, Fla.: Rourke Enterprises, Inc., 1988.

Epler, Doris M. *The Berlin Wall: How It Rose and Why It Fell*. Brookfield, Conn.: The Millbrook Press, 1992.

Fritzsche, Peter and Karen Hewitt. *Berlinwalks*. New York: Henry Holt and Company, 1994.

Holland, Jack and John Gawthrop. *Berlin: The Rough Guide*. London: The Rough Guides, 1995.

McLachlan, Gordon. *Berlin: Capital of the New Germany*. Lincolnwood, Ill.: Passport Books, 1995.

Steins, Richard. *Berlin*. The Great Cities Library series. New York: Blackbird Press, 1991.

Tucker, Alan (ed.). *The Berlitz Travellers Guide to Berlin*. New York: Berlitz Publishing Company, Inc., 1993.

Yancy, Diane. *The Reunification of Germany*. World in Conflict series. San Diego: Lucent Books, Inc., 1994.

ONLINE SITES

Berlin
http://www.chemie.fu-berlin.de/adressen/berlin.html
A brief history of Berlin and the Berlin Wall, as well as lots of information on Germany and links to other sites.

The Berlin-Bear
http://www.berlin-bear.de/BBear/home.html
Art galleries, the zoo, a city guide, weather reports, museums, and history. This site jumps from English to German without warning.

The Berlin Wall Falls
http://www.educat.hu-berlin.de/~stefan/mauer/
Stories and pictures, by teenagers, of life with the Wall—and how things changed after it came down.

German Historical Museum
http://www.dhm.de/
Information about museums, exhibitions, collections, and history. See postcards and toys from the 1800s. Links to other museums.

German Map
http://www.leo.org/demap/
Select any of more than one hundred German cities—each with dozens of links.

Germany
http://www.fal.de/english/germany/brd-fact.html
Every fact and figure about Germany you can imagine—from land area to climate, from population to languages, from history to ethnic divisions, political leaders, the economy, and much more.

LTU International Airways Travel Guide to Germany
http://www.ltu.com/ltu
Mostly text, but a ton of information. After wandering around this site, you'll feel as though you've been to Germany's biggest and most historic cities. From the home page, click on "Travel Guide to Germany."

The Webfoot's Guide to Germany
http://www.webfoot.com/travel/guides/germany/germany.html
Links to a factbook, satellite weather images, German money, maps, the current time, a virtual library, and more.

ABOUT THE AUTHOR

R. Conrad Stein was born and grew up in Chicago. After serving in the Marine Corps, he attended the University of Illinois, where he received a degree in history. He has published more than eighty books for young readers. Mr. Stein lives in Chicago with his wife and their daughter Janna.